Hello, Family Members,

Learning to read is one of the most important accomplishments of early childhood. **Hello Reader!** books are designed to help children become skilled readers who like to read. Beginning readers learn to read by remembering frequently used words like "the," "is," and "and"; by using phonics skills to decode new words; and by interpreting picture and text clues. These books provide both the stories children enjoy and the structure they need to read fluently and independently. Here are suggestions for helping your child *before*, *during*, and *after* reading:

Before

- Look at the cover and pictures and have your child predict what the story is about.
- Read the story to your child.
- Encourage your child to chime in with familiar words and phrases.
- Echo read with your child by reading a line first and having your child read it after you do.

During

- Have your child think about a word he or she does not recognize right away. Provide hints such as "Let's see if we know the sounds" and "Have we read other words like this one?"
- Encourage your child to use phonics skills to sound out new words.
- Provide the word for your child when more assistance is needed so that he or she does not struggle and the experience of reading with you is a positive one.
- Encourage your child to have fun by reading with a lot of expression . . . like an actor!

After

- Have your child keep lists of interesting and favorite words.
- Encourage your child to read the books over and over again. Have him or her read to brothers, sisters, grandparents, and even teddy bears. Repeated readings develop confidence in young readers.
- Talk about the stories. Ask and answer questions. Share ideas about the funniest and most interesting characters and events in the stories.

I do hope that you and your child enjoy this book.

—Francie Alexander
  Reading Specialist,
  Scholastic's Learning Ventures

For Heidi, Bea, and Maddie—
three in the sea!
—P.R. and C.R.

For my new niece, Maryann
—C.S.

Text copyright © 2000 by Peter and Connie Roop.
Illustrations copyright © 2000 by Carol Schwartz.
All rights reserved. Published by Scholastic Inc.
SCHOLASTIC, HELLO READER, CARTWHEEL BOOKS and associated logos
are trademarks and/or registered trademarks of Scholastic Inc.

Library of Congress Cataloging-in-Publication Data
Roop, Peter.
   Whales and dolphins / by Peter and Connie Roop; illustrated by Carol Schwartz.
   p. cm. — (Hello reader! Science—Level 1)
   "Cartwheel books."
   Summary: Simple rhyming text describes the behavior of whales and dolphins, including
singing, diving, playing, and eating.
   ISBN 0-439-09912-9
      1. Cetacea—juvenile literature . [1. Whales. 2. Dolphins.] I. Title II. Schwartz, Carol,
1954- ill. III. Roop, Connie.
   QL737.C4R59 2000
   599.5 21—dc21   99-041766

10 9 8 7 6 5 4 3   00 01 02 03 04

Whales and Dolphins

by Peter and Connie Roop
Illustrated by Carol Schwartz

Hello Reader! Science — Level 1

SCHOLASTIC INC.

New York Toronto London Auckland Sydney Mexico City New Delhi Hong Kong

Whales and dolphins swim,
just like you and me.

Whales and dolphins leap
high above the sea.

Whales and dolphins eat,
as we do every day.

Whales and dolphins sleep
in their underwater way.

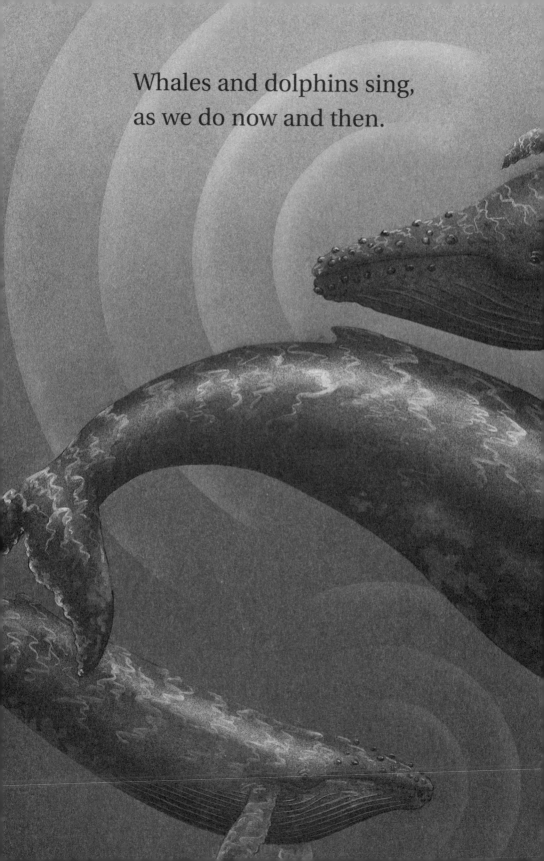

Whales and dolphins sing,
as we do now and then.

Whales and dolphins play,
then splash and swim again.

Just like you and me,
whales and dolphins dive.

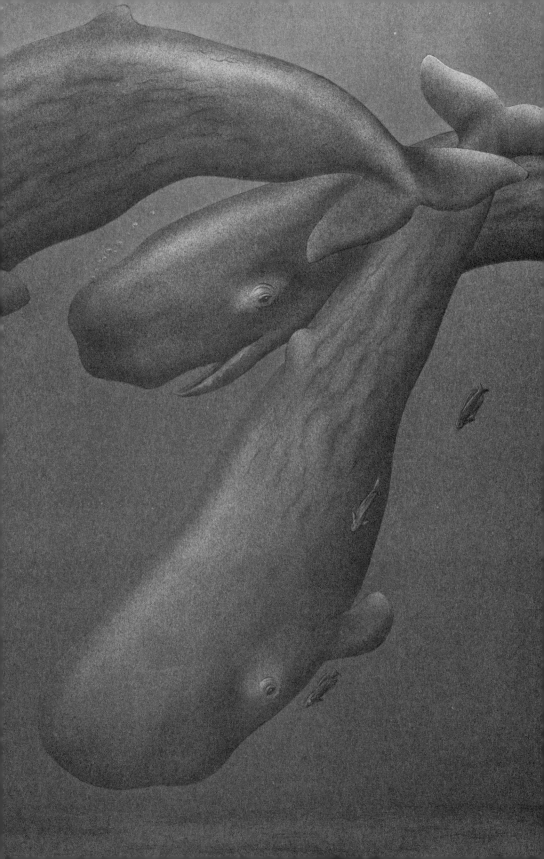

And they breathe the air we do
that keeps us all alive.

Whales and dolphins sip
their mother's milk,
the same way that we do.

Whales and dolphins are mammals.
That's what we are, too!

They swim...
they leap...
they eat...
they sleep...
under the same blue sky.

They sing…
they play…
they dive…
they breathe…
the same as you and I.

Whales and dolphins share the earth from their home in the sea.

Whales and dolphins share our world...

together with you and me.